Community Helpers

Chefs

by Cari Meister

Bullfrog Books

Ideas for Parents and Teachers

Bullfrog Books let children practice reading informational text at the earliest reading levels. Repetition, familiar words, and photo labels support early readers.

Before Reading
- Discuss the cover photo. What does it tell them?
- Look at the picture glossary together. Read and discuss the words.

Read the Book
- "Walk" through the book and look at the photos. Let the child ask questions. Point out the photo labels.
- Read the book to the child, or have him or her read independently.

After Reading
- Prompt the child to think more. Ask: Where have you seen a chef? What was he or she cooking?

Bullfrog Books are published by Jump!
5357 Penn Avenue South
Minneapolis, MN 55419
www.jumplibrary.com

Library of Congress Cataloging-in-Publication Data
Meister, Cari, author.
  Chefs / by Cari Meister.
    pages cm. —(Community helpers) (Bullfrog books)
  Summary: "This photo-illustrated book for early readers explains the different kinds of chefs who work in a restaurant and what they do" —Provided by publisher.
  Includes bibliographical references and index.
  ISBN 978-1-62031-089-2 (hardcover)
  ISBN 978-1-62496-157-1 (ebook)
  ISBN 978-1-62031-133-2 (paperback)
  1. Cooks —Juvenile literature. I. Title.
  TX652.5.M3577 2015
  641.5'092 —dc23
                                    2013037884

Editor: Wendy Dieker
Series Designer: Ellen Huber
Book Designer: Lindaanne Donohoe
Photo Researcher: Kurtis Kinneman

Photo Credits: All photos by Shutterstock except Alamy 6-7, 10-11; Dreamstime 12, 21, Cafe Maude 7, 23bl; Superstock 4

Printed in the United States of America at Corporate Graphics, North Mankato, Minnesota.
6-2014
10 9 8 7 6 5 4 3 2 1

Table of Contents

Chefs at Work

Ed wants to be a chef.

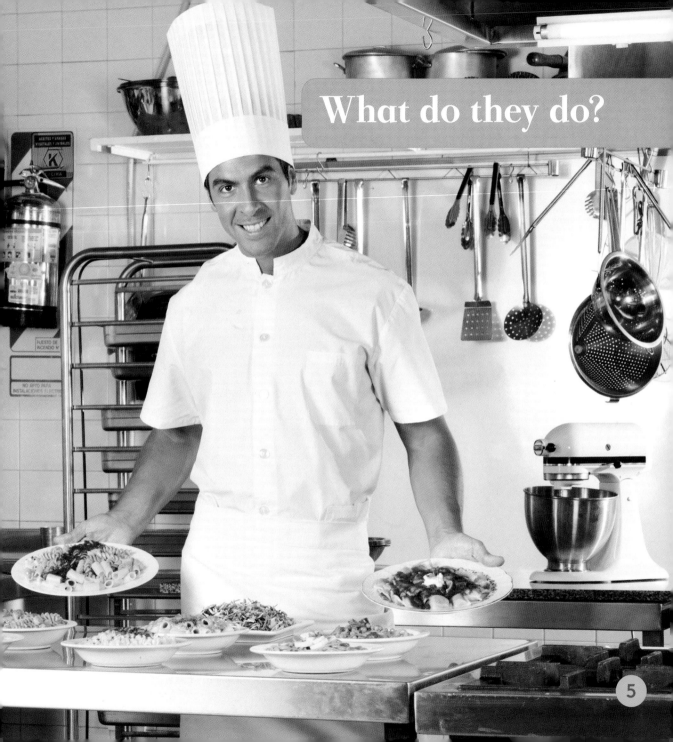

What do they do?

They plan menus.
They make food.

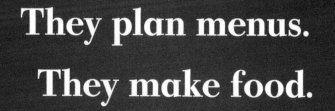

menu

A chef buys food.
She will cook a good meal.

Li works in a
restaurant.

He is the head chef.

He is the boss.

Al is next in charge.

He cooks the lamb.

12

It needs salt.
There!
It is ready.

lamb

13

Sun makes a salad.

She cuts.

She chops.

Yum!

TJ makes the sauce.

He stirs.

He tastes.

Mm! Done!

sauce

pastry
bag

Kim makes a cake.

She has a pastry bag.

It has a tip.

It can make a flower.

Pretty!

Chefs do good work!

In the Kitchen

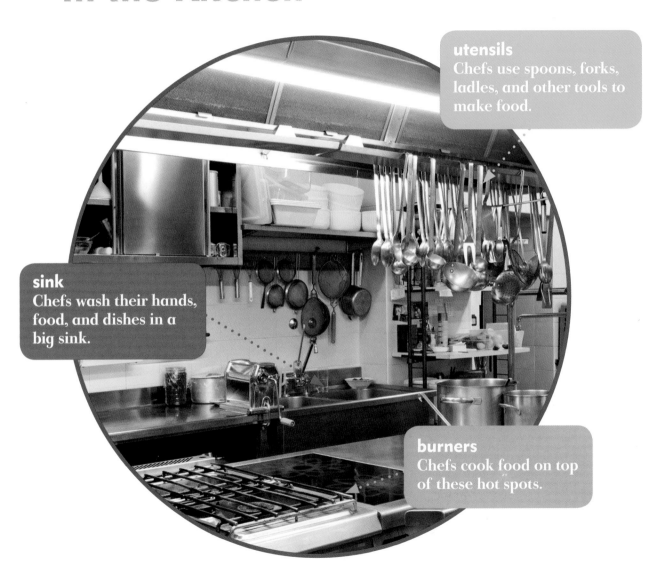

utensils
Chefs use spoons, forks, ladles, and other tools to make food.

sink
Chefs wash their hands, food, and dishes in a big sink.

burners
Chefs cook food on top of these hot spots.

Picture Glossary

head chef
The chef in charge of all of the other chefs.

pastry bag
A bag that holds frosting. Chefs squeeze it to make decorations.

menu
A list of the food served at a restaurant.

sauce
A thick liquid served with food, like gravy.

Index

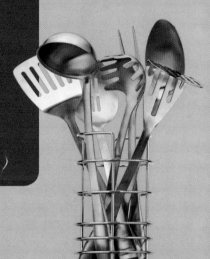

To Learn More

Learning more is as easy as 1, 2, 3.

1) Go to www.factsurfer.com

2) Enter "chefs" into the search box.

3) Click the "Surf" button to see a list of websites.

With factsurfer.com, finding more information is just a click away.